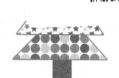 

# THIS BOOK BELONGS TO

---

PHONE NUMBER

---

EMAIL

---

NAME

GIFT IDEAS

BUDGET                     ACTUAL

STORE/GIFT

☐ ORDERED?    ☐ WRAPPED?    ☐ SENT/GIVEN

NOTES

NAME

GIFT IDEAS

BUDGET                    ACTUAL

STORE/GIFT

☐ ORDERED?        ☐ WRAPPED?        ☐ SENT/GIVEN?

NOTES

NAME

GIFT IDEAS

BUDGET					ACTUAL

STORE/GIFT

☐ ORDERED?			☐ WRAPPED?			☐ SENT/GIVEN?

## NOTES

NAME

GIFT IDEAS

BUDGET                    ACTUAL

STORE/GIFT

☐ ORDERED?        ☐ WRAPPED?        ☐ SENT/GIVEN?

🌿 NOTES 🌿

NAME

GIFT IDEAS

BUDGET    ACTUAL

STORE/GIFT

☐ ORDERED?    ☐ WRAPPED?    ☐ SENT/GIVEN?

🍂 NOTES 🍂

NAME

GIFT IDEAS

BUDGET                    ACTUAL

STORE/GIFT

☐ ORDERED?      ☐ WRAPPED?       ☐ SENT/GIVEN?

### NOTES

NAME

GIFT IDEAS

BUDGET                    ACTUAL

STORE/GIFT

☐ ORDERED?    ☐ WRAPPED?    ☐ SENT/GIVEN

🌿 NOTES 🌿

NAME

GIFT IDEAS

BUDGET          ACTUAL

STORE/GIFT

☐ ORDERED?    ☐ WRAPPED?    ☐ SENT/GIVEN?

🍁 NOTES 🍁

NAME

GIFT IDEAS

BUDGET                    ACTUAL

STORE/GIFT

☐ ORDERED?        ☐ WRAPPED?        ☐ SENT/GIVEN?

🍂 NOTES 🍂

NAME

GIFT IDEAS

BUDGET                    ACTUAL

STORE/GIFT

☐ ORDERED?        ☐ WRAPPED?        ☐ SENT/GIVEN?

🍂 NOTES 🍂

# NAME

# GIFT IDEAS

# BUDGET          ACTUAL

# STORE/GIFT

☐ ORDERED?    ☐ WRAPPED?    ☐ SENT/GIVEN?

## 🍂 NOTES 🍂

NAME

GIFT IDEAS

BUDGET                    ACTUAL

STORE/GIFT

☐ ORDERED?    ☐ WRAPPED?    ☐ SENT/GIVEN?

❧ NOTES ❧

NAME

GIFT IDEAS

BUDGET                    ACTUAL

STORE/GIFT

☐ ORDERED?        ☐ WRAPPED?         ☐ SENT/GIVEN

🌿 NOTES 🌿

NAME

GIFT IDEAS

BUDGET                    ACTUAL

STORE/GIFT

☐ ORDERED?        ☐ WRAPPED?        ☐ SENT/GIVEN?

🍂 NOTES 🍂

NAME

GIFT IDEAS

BUDGET    ACTUAL

STORE/GIFT

☐ ORDERED?    ☐ WRAPPED?    ☐ SENT/GIVEN?

NOTES

NAME

GIFT IDEAS

BUDGET                    ACTUAL

STORE/GIFT

☐ ORDERED?        ☐ WRAPPED?        ☐ SENT/GIVEN?

NOTES

NAME

GIFT IDEAS

BUDGET                    ACTUAL

STORE/GIFT

☐ ORDERED?        ☐ WRAPPED?        ☐ SENT/GIVEN?

🍁 NOTES 🍁

NAME

GIFT IDEAS

BUDGET                          ACTUAL

STORE/GIFT

☐ ORDERED?        ☐ WRAPPED?        ☐ SENT/GIVEN?

NOTES

NAME

GIFT IDEAS

BUDGET         ACTUAL

STORE/GIFT

☐ ORDERED?   ☐ WRAPPED?   ☐ SENT/GIVEN

🌿 NOTES 🌿

NAME

GIFT IDEAS

BUDGET	ACTUAL

STORE/GIFT

☐ ORDERED?  ☐ WRAPPED?  ☐ SENT/GIVEN?

### 🍃 NOTES 🍃

NAME

GIFT IDEAS

BUDGET                    ACTUAL

STORE/GIFT

☐ ORDERED?        ☐ WRAPPED?        ☐ SENT/GIVEN?

🌿 NOTES 🌿

NAME

GIFT IDEAS

BUDGET                                ACTUAL

STORE/GIFT

☐ ORDERED?           ☐ WRAPPED?           ☐ SENT/GIVEN?

❦ NOTES ❦

NAME

GIFT IDEAS

BUDGET                    ACTUAL

STORE/GIFT

☐ ORDERED?     ☐ WRAPPED?     ☐ SENT/GIVEN?

🍁 NOTES 🍁

NAME

GIFT IDEAS

BUDGET                         ACTUAL

STORE/GIFT

☐ ORDERED?        ☐ WRAPPED?        ☐ SENT/GIVEN?

❦ NOTES ❦

NAME

GIFT IDEAS

BUDGET                ACTUAL

STORE/GIFT

☐ ORDERED?     ☐ WRAPPED?     ☐ SENT/GIVEN

🍃 NOTES 🍃

NAME

GIFT IDEAS

BUDGET                    ACTUAL

STORE/GIFT

☐ ORDERED?      ☐ WRAPPED?      ☐ SENT/GIVEN?

🍁 NOTES 🍁

NAME

GIFT IDEAS

BUDGET　　　　　　　ACTUAL

STORE/GIFT

☐ ORDERED?　　☐ WRAPPED?　　☐ SENT/GIVEN?

### NOTES

NAME

GIFT IDEAS

BUDGET                    ACTUAL

STORE/GIFT

☐ ORDERED?        ☐ WRAPPED?         ☐ SENT/GIVEN?

### NOTES

NAME

GIFT IDEAS

BUDGET					ACTUAL

STORE/GIFT

☐ ORDERED?		☐ WRAPPED?		☐ SENT/GIVEN?

🌿 NOTES 🌿

NAME

GIFT IDEAS

BUDGET                    ACTUAL

STORE/GIFT

☐ ORDERED?        ☐ WRAPPED?        ☐ SENT/GIVEN?

🍂 NOTES 🍂

NAME

GIFT IDEAS

BUDGET                    ACTUAL

STORE/GIFT

☐ ORDERED?    ☐ WRAPPED?    ☐ SENT/GIVEN

🌿 NOTES 🌿

NAME

GIFT IDEAS

BUDGET               ACTUAL

STORE/GIFT

☐ ORDERED?      ☐ WRAPPED?      ☐ SENT/GIVEN?

NOTES

NAME

GIFT IDEAS

BUDGET                    ACTUAL

STORE/GIFT

☐ ORDERED?        ☐ WRAPPED?         ☐ SENT/GIVEN?

NOTES

NAME

GIFT IDEAS

BUDGET    ACTUAL

STORE/GIFT

☐ ORDERED?    ☐ WRAPPED?    ☐ SENT/GIVEN?

🍂 NOTES 🍂

NAME

GIFT IDEAS

BUDGET                    ACTUAL

STORE/GIFT

☐ ORDERED?     ☐ WRAPPED?     ☐ SENT/GIVEN?

NOTES

NAME

GIFT IDEAS

BUDGET                ACTUAL

STORE/GIFT

☐ ORDERED?        ☐ WRAPPED?        ☐ SENT/GIVEN?

NOTES

NAME

GIFT IDEAS

BUDGET  ACTUAL

STORE/GIFT

☐ ORDERED?   ☐ WRAPPED?   ☐ SENT/GIVEN

🌿 NOTES 🌿

NAME

GIFT IDEAS

BUDGET                    ACTUAL

STORE/GIFT

☐ ORDERED?        ☐ WRAPPED?        ☐ SENT/GIVEN?

🌿 NOTES 🌿

NAME

GIFT IDEAS

BUDGET	ACTUAL

STORE/GIFT

☐ ORDERED?	☐ WRAPPED?	☐ SENT/GIVEN?

❦ NOTES ❦

NAME

GIFT IDEAS

BUDGET　　　　　　ACTUAL

STORE/GIFT

☐ ORDERED?　　☐ WRAPPED?　　☐ SENT/GIVEN?

NOTES

NAME

GIFT IDEAS

BUDGET                              ACTUAL

STORE/GIFT

☐ ORDERED?        ☐ WRAPPED?         ☐ SENT/GIVEN?

🍂 NOTES 🍂

NAME

GIFT IDEAS

BUDGET                                    ACTUAL

STORE/GIFT

☐ ORDERED?          ☐ WRAPPED?          ☐ SENT/GIVEN?

🍂 NOTES 🍂

| NAME | |
|---|---|

| GIFT IDEAS | |
|---|---|

| BUDGET | ACTUAL |
|---|---|

| STORE/GIFT | |
|---|---|

☐ ORDERED?  ☐ WRAPPED?  ☐ SENT/GIVEN

🌿 NOTES 🌿

NAME

GIFT IDEAS

BUDGET                    ACTUAL

STORE/GIFT

☐ ORDERED?        ☐ WRAPPED?        ☐ SENT/GIVEN?

NOTES

NAME

GIFT IDEAS

BUDGET                          ACTUAL

STORE/GIFT

☐ ORDERED?        ☐ WRAPPED?        ☐ SENT/GIVEN?

🍁 NOTES 🍁

NAME

GIFT IDEAS

BUDGET                          ACTUAL

STORE/GIFT

☐ ORDERED?        ☐ WRAPPED?         ☐ SENT/GIVEN?

🍂 NOTES 🍂

NAME

GIFT IDEAS

BUDGET					ACTUAL

STORE/GIFT

☐ ORDERED?		☐ WRAPPED?		☐ SENT/GIVEN?

## NOTES

NAME

GIFT IDEAS

BUDGET					ACTUAL

STORE/GIFT

☐ ORDERED?		☐ WRAPPED?		☐ SENT/GIVEN?

### ❦ NOTES ❦

Made in United States
Orlando, FL
03 December 2024